I Will Do My Best

Gemma's Journey to Success

I love you Emma! ♡ xoxo

Skoufis

Written by Nathan Skoufis

Illustrated by Maruf Hasan

BOOKBILDR PUBLISHING

First published in the USA in 2024 by BookBildr Publishing.

The moral rights of the author and illustrator have been asserted.

ISBN 978-1-964012-27-8

Text copyright ©2024 by Nathan Skoufis

BookBildr Publishing

An imprint of BookBildr LLC

7901 4th St N, Suite 300

St. Petersburg, FL, 33702

USA

www.bookbildr.com

This book belongs to

Gemma was in class and looked over at the other students practising their moves.

"They are so awesome and I will never be able to do that," she thought.

Gemma sighed and looked down at her feet. She knew she should get back to practise but… she felt tired and sad.

"Gemma," her Sensei called out. "Is everything OK? Are you ready to practise some more?"

"Ummm… I still feel tired," Gemma replied quietly, without looking up.

Sensei Nathan walked over and asked, "Are you feeling OK? You seem quiet lately."

"Why can't I be as good as the other kids?" Gemma exclaimed and pointed to the other students. "I really try but it's just so hard! I understand what I need to do but when I try, I can't get the moves right."

She was almost crying and felt ashamed. "Why can't I kick as high as the other students?" she added quietly.

"Come," said Sensei Nathan and walked over to the trophy display. "All these trophies belong to our students. I was hoping to see yours here one day."

Gemma looked at the trophies. She didn't know what to say - she never thought her Sensei had so much trust in her.

"You know," Sensei Nathan continued. "Karate is more than just punching and kicking. It's a lot like real life and life can be hard. Sometimes giving up feels like an easy solution but it is not. If you keep trying your best and teach yourself perseverance, one day all your hard work will pay off and you'll succeed. But it's not going to happen overnight. You see, Gemma, I like to think every student is like a snowflake - all are unique and beautiful in their own way. It is all about trying your personal best. Through karate, we learn to overcome obstacles and understand that it might not always be easy to reach our goals. But it's definitely worth it."

"I understand, Sensei. I will keep trying my best. I will not compare myself to other students because I am like a snowflake!" said Gemma.

"Great! The tournament for your age group is in two months. I think you can make it," said Sensei Nathan.

Suddenly, getting sweaty and tired didn't matter anymore to Gemma. She was having fun working on her moves in class.

Gemma practised every day. When things didn't work out, she took a deep breath and tried again. *I will not give up, I will do my best,* she kept saying to herself. Soon she got stronger, faster, and her moves improved tremendously.

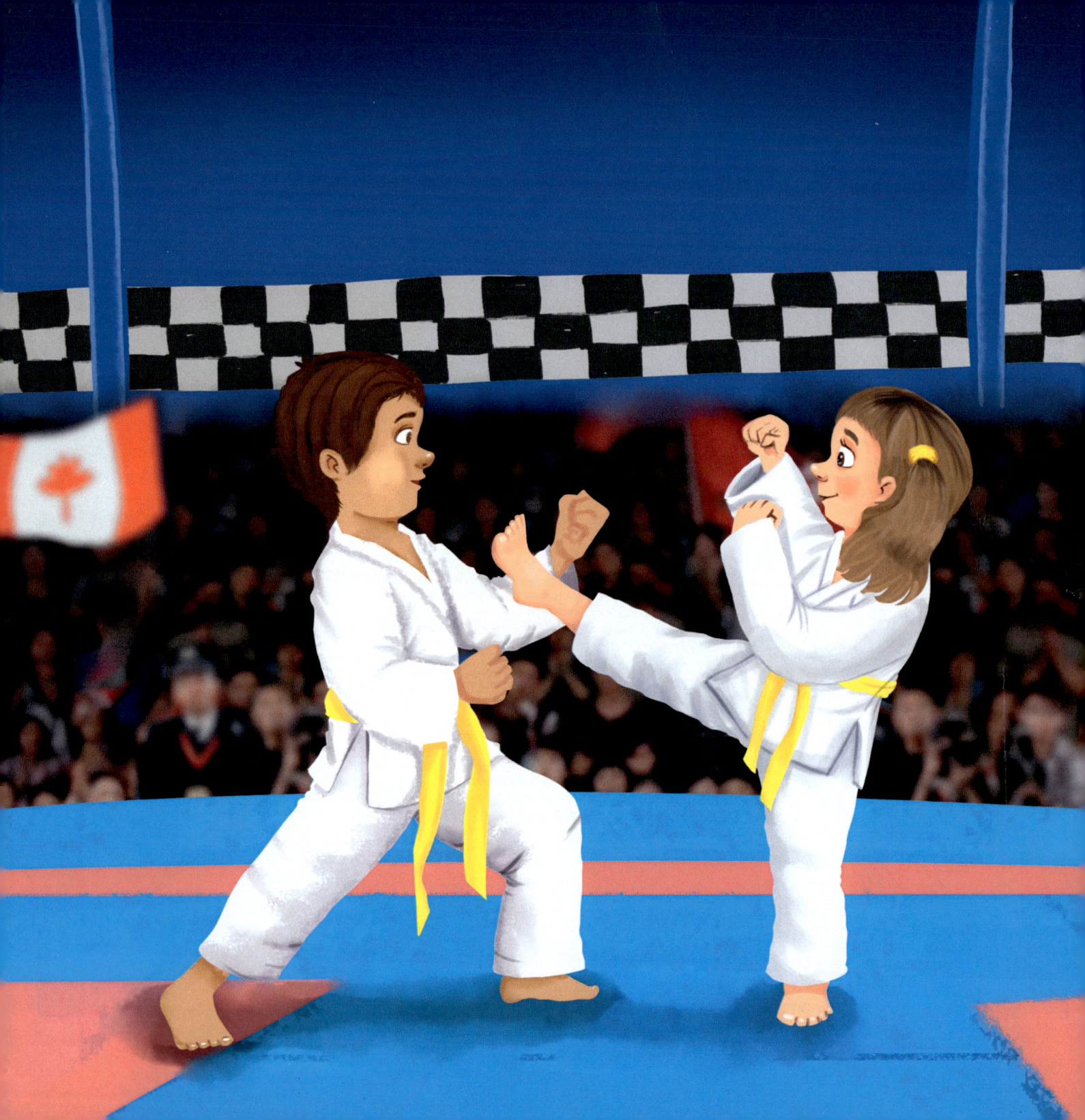

At the tournament, her opponents were very good. But every time things got tough, Gemma said to herself, *I will do my best and have fun like Sensei Nathan told me.*

Gemma made it to the finals and then something amazing happened - the referee announced her as the winner and handed her the trophy. Gemma was delighted.

Everyone cheered, "Congratulations, Gemma!!"

When things quietened down, Gemma bowed to Sensei Nathan and gave him a big hug. "Thank you for teaching me not to give up, Sensei Nathan", said Gemma.

Sensei Nathan returned the bow and said, "I am so proud of you for overcoming this challenge."

About the Author

Nathan Skoufis is a 25x World Martial Arts Champion, 6th Degree Black Belt, and member of Team Canada. A sport that he started at the age of four, having claimed several international gold medals for Canada.

He is the owner and Head Instructor of Guelph Family Martial Arts and Guelph Fitness Kickboxing.

His studio was selected as the top studio in the country for its positive impact on students of all ages. Nathan was also recognized as the top trainer in the country.

Nathan works with students of all ages, from as young as three years old to over 70 years old. He is a motivational speaker for a variety of events to help share his story. He works with students with varying learning challenges including those on the autistic spectrum.

Nathan utilizes training as a vehicle to facilitate personal development and growth and to instill powerful life lessons of perseverance, confidence, and many more. His studio is a fun and nonjudgmental environment where everyone can feel welcome and thrive to their fullest potential.

Nathan is heavily involved in the area in a number of charity and community organizations where he sparks positive growth in the community. He has been an ambassador for several organizations in his community.

In his children's books, Sensei Nathan wants to share the core principles of martial arts and encourage children to always do their best in whatever they are doing. Martial arts have changed his life and Nathan wants to share that with everyone.

Manufactured by Amazon.ca
Bolton, ON

41309062R00017